VINTAGE 1999

Vintage 1999 is an anthology of the best poems from
the 1999 National Poetry Contest and the Canadian Youth Poetry
Competiton. Entry details for the contests may be
found at the end of the volume.

The National Poetry Contest
1999 Prize Winners

FIRST PRIZE: Susan Stenson
"When You Say Infidelity"

SECOND PRIZE: Peter Richardson
"Dig"

THIRD PRIZE: Brent MacLaine
"Southward to Kissimmee"

The Canadian Youth Poetry Competition
1999 Prize Winners

Senior Division

FIRST PRIZE: Jessie Carson
"Space Between Our Fingers"

SECOND PRIZE: Julia Thompson
"Pomegranates"

THIRD PRIZE: Ami Drummond
"Corn Nuts on the Back Seat"

Junior Division

FIRST PRIZE: Fabienne Calvert-Filteau
"Four Ways to Look at Nai Nai's
Growth Chart"

SECOND PRIZE: Anne Gaspar
"A Tree"

THIRD PRIZE: Marena Winstanley
"The Politics of the School: Utensils"

VINTAGE 1999

poems from

The National
Poetry Contest

&

The Canadian Youth
Poetry Competition

THE LEAGUE
of CANADIAN
POETS

RONSDALE PRESS
1999

VINTAGE 1999
Copyright © 1999 League of Canadian Poets

RONSDALE PRESS LTD.
3350 West 21st Avenue
Vancouver, B.C., Canada
V6S 1G7

Set in New Baskerville: 10.5 pt on 13.5
Typesetting: Julie Cochrane
Printing: Hignell Printing, Winnipeg, Manitoba
Cover Art: Joe Plaskett, detail of *Provincetown Cemetery*, 1948, Watercolour, 13" x 19"
Cover Design: Julie Cochrane

Ronsdale Press wishes to thank the Canada Council for the Arts, the Government of Canada through the Book Publishing Industry Development Program (BPIDP), and the Province of British Columbia through the British Columbia Arts Council for their support of its publishing program.

ISBN: 0-921870-70-1

CANADIAN CATALOGUING IN PUBLICATION DATA

Main entry under title:

Vintage

ISSN 1204-4504

1. Canadian poetry (English) — 20th century.* I. League of Canadian Poets.
PS8279.V55   C811'.5408'005   C96-300232-5
PR9195.25.V55

Contents

Foreword

Each year the League of Canadian Poets sponsors the National Poetry Competition and the Youth Poetry Competition. Both have as their aim the encouragement of poetic talent.

The National Poetry Competion has been an annual event ever since its beginning in 1986 and is now one of Canada's most prestigious writing competitions, offering all Canadians a chance to discover their writing abilities. Six well known poets are selected by the League's National Council to judge the contest. The judgement criterion is straight forward: quality of writing. Each year the 50 winning poems of the National Poetry Contest are gathered into the poetry anthology *Vintage*. From these poems, the top three are chosen and cash prizes of $1,000, $750 and $500 are awarded.

The Canadian Youth Poetry Competition comprises two categories: the junior division for students in grades 7 to 9, and the senior division for grades 10 to 12 (OAC in Ontario). The judges are established poets who choose the top three poems in each category, with cash prizes of $500, $300 and $250 for each category. There are also a number of honourable mentions. The three prize poems in each category are included in *Vintage*.

Vintage 1999, published by Ronsdale Press, is available at book stores across Canada and also directly from the League of Canadian Poets. With poets represented from all over Canada and all age groups, *Vintage 1999* represents a broad range of writing styles and topics and offers an ideal introduction to the vitality and diversity of Canadian poetry.

The National
Poetry Contest

Introduction to the National Poetry Contest

Judges: Joe Blades, Susan Ingersoll, Brian Bartlett,
        Michael Harris, Carolyn Zonailo, Jennifer Boire

One of the unfortunate things about contests is that one has to choose a winner. Without reservation we were able to agree on fifty poems that really stood out, in both quality of writing and in their ability to move us. However, we trust that what will be evident in our final choice of the top three poems is their unique combination of fine writing and good craft, the poets' willingness to take risks with their subject matter and — the cornerstone of all excellent writing — insight.

What we appreciate in "When You Say Infidelity" by Susan Stenson, is its delicate balancing of craft and content. The writing itself is accomplished, but what recommends this poem to us in particular is the poet's handling of the extended poetic conceit, involving a complex mixing of imagery, emotion and suggestion. The poem is both subtle in its conception and realization, and unabashedly forthright in its dealing with this difficult part of the realm of human experience.

What astonishes in Peter Richardson's "Dig" is the laconic clarity of the writing. Although the subject matter is not pleasant, the actual experience of reading the poem is aesthetically gratifying despite the poem's immediacy. It also contains a larger subtext bringing in nuances of domestic relationships. The poem's economy of language and emotions resonates.

Brent MacLaine's "Southward to Kissimmee" is a clear-headed take on the decline of a family member, rendered with subtle passion all the while steering clear of sentimentality. The writing stays fresh, while dealing with its theme of loss. It is a perfectly realized narrative, embellished with particularly felicitous images and insights.

— Michael Harris
Carolyn Zonailo
Jennifer Boire

The National Poetry Contest
1999 Prize Winners

Susan Stenson
"When You Say Infidelity"

SECOND PRIZE
Peter Richardson
"Dig"

THIRD PRIZE
Brent MacLaine
"Southward to Kissimmee"

When You Say Infidelity

it sounds like something in the garden
planted beside foxglove, forget-me-not.
It is not beautiful
but your friends will recognize
the stems and furry leaves, hungover,
may even whisper its Latin name.
How would we classify it?
A border plant?
One that prefers shade?
How to describe the bloom?
The species you are most likely to find
thrives anywhere, the guidebooks will say
under the cozy light of a neighbour's kitchen,
in Best Westerns, close to the nearest exit,
at the party where I play
piano. Upstairs on a guest bed
I find you with a friend, I'll call Margery.
My Margery. If it were a movie,
I could close my eyes.
Later walk in the garden.
Margery planting roots
in that hard place between
the heart and a bad day
or above the trellis
thin and reserved in this light
where infidelity now hangs.

Dig

She must've worked it out the way
you'd fetch the knotted drawstring
partway out of a pair of stretchpants,
pinching off a bit of the material
at a time, coaxing the cord's end
backwards towards the drawhole
then reaching in with tweezers
for the knot, or, in this case, the end
of my left ring finger, snipped off
while I bent over to check
the front doorsill lock of a DC-10.
That would be something to see:
a full half-inch of severed digit
brought to light by stages after
spoiling a perfectly good glove.
How could she pass that up after
noting the glove in our hall closet
in the pocket of my work parka,
a fortnight into my convalescence?
This woman who has trouble
watching an ant being flattened,
who scolds when I clap my hands
to make crows fly up from our lawn,
maneuvers the pulp backwards
towards the glove's elasticized top,
letting it plop into the toilet, where
she notes for my averted gaze
the little white filament of nerve
trailing out behind it like a vestigial
tail on a new kind of pollywog.

Southward to Kissimmee

I

Our preference was for you to mellow
in well heated rooms. We would see
to the vegetables — keep them dry
in the cellar beneath the dining room,
and during our visits we would watch
your drop cookies congealing as they cooled.
We expected you to tolerate your fate
the way you would an uninvited guest —
civilly with cubes of cheddar cheese
on cracker rounds, with last year's
Christmas cake and lots of well boiled tea.
We thought that you would ease
yourself compliantly into a lazy-boy
with pockets for fliers and crossword books.
Reclining there would make it easier
to watch the nightly news, and even
as the world declined before your dimming
eyes, at least we knew that with
a calmly aimed remote, you could
flick aside the crime, the burning,
and all the faces of the day's destruction.

II

Instead,
your imagination shatters daily
into image bits that whirl like fortune's wheel
and ratchet by us louder than our reasonable voices.
Your perturbations spin like lottery balls
flung into prizeless sequences.
We ought to have known that you would kaleidoscope the world,

that you would run from the yellowish glow of sweet-sad memory,
lacy and strong as antiques to the nose.
Can we blame you for cursing the softness of carpets
vacuumed when they needn't be?
Comfort may be the last thing on your mind.

So, go ahead, let your distractions fly,
ragged and streamered as the clutter of sales
in mega-stores and malls.
Or over rye and ginger on a Saturday night
with neighbours telling naughty jokes,
we wish you a really good Legion band.

What do we know of the loss,
the oh, so tremendous loss of never again
in January loading up a floaty Ford
and heading southward to Kissimmee,
befriending desk clerks at cheap motels all along the coast?

Two *Bathshebas* in the Louvre*

I.

The breasts make contact with you first, the face —
pretty, oh yes — recedes into the unseen, as
the red eyes of the breasts
invite
floodlight on her deshabille.
If she can read
you wouldn't know it,
pretty earrings too
a shoulder to be lightly
brushed
yes, you'll take this one
she says "take me" — letter from her dead past
dangling from her little hand — she says
"Only *you* exist
now, *you're* the king
take me" —
a real pin-up this one and you'll
take her
(sucker).

II.

Someone kneeling
to wash a woman's feet, that's all
some androgynous old domestic, maybe,
head covered in cardinal
red and the woman entirely
naked, not
nude, you can't not
look at her
face

and beyond the face
an entirely naked
woman and you can't not
look
on her private, not
to be spoken thought, you can't
take her, you're
with her in her knowing
solitude, in the space
where two sometimes stay
beside one another, not
fleeing, not
speaking, in the space
where it can't be
helped
you lower yourself
to see, you
listen with your eyes, you
watch a man entirely
helpless, tender, powerful,
kneel
at his companion's feet
to take her
flesh in his hands and brush
her with his
painter's
consolation

She supports her weight
on one large, ringless hand (you know
those wailing fingers) she's been
nailed
by the letter the other hand holds, its corner
clotted with the king's seal. Not
a young thing — her widened navel that,
despite yourself, you look to as an

eye, has been stretched.
Her body won't let you
forget its past, a body made
in time, for all time,
Bathsheba between men, between
masters, Bathsheba,
(*"Oh Hendrickje!"*)
(and you), by this painter
faithfully
beloved.

---

* The first painting, "Bathsheba Reading a Letter from David," is by Willem Drost
(known only as Rembrandt's pupil) c.1630-1680. The second was painted by Rem-
brandt in 1654. Hendrickje Stoffels, Rembrandt's housekeeper, and the model for
this work, was charged that same year by the Council of the Reformed Church
with having "shamed herself by fornication with Rembrandt" and was forbidden
to take communion.

Frieze of Life

"Birth and Life at the Fin de Siècle —
Symbolist Europe: Lost Paradise"

My daughter found her favourite painting
pasted on fences and walls all over Montréal —
Klimt's "Hope I": the naked pregnant woman
in profile with her head turned to the viewer,
and a skull and scowling faces in the upper margin.
I had Cate stand outside the Musée des Beaux Arts
by that poster, so that I could take her picture.
She looks up, her eyes closed in the sunlight.
The museum shop had the ultimate kitsch souvenir,
an inflatable model of Munch's "The Scream",
part of his *Frieze of Life* series, Berlin,
1902. It would be a pleasure to buy
the little inflatable grotesque
and let it deflate with an ignoble noise,
the distorted face distorting further.
A candidate for picture of the century?
Or do we go with the shyness under threat
of Klimt's pregnant redhead, painted the year
after Munch's howling cartoon? My favourite Klimt
is "Schubert at the Piano". The candles
have turned the women's dresses to light
as they stand listening in the fragile spell of art.
Schubert sits in a band of shadow in the picture.
Painted two years before the new century, it failed
to outlive it. *1945 Verbrannt,* the reproduction says.

My photograph has no threatening margins:
my own child is my best symbol of hope.

Four Hungry Sisters

For all our differences,
we have the same pink mouth,
open and wanting more.
We have all eaten one thing dangerous,
one thing regretted.

Josephine is the sensible one
and should have been the oldest.
She crunched on tangy ants
like lemon drops
their feelers tickling her tongue.

On a dare, Adrien swallowed
a centipede we called the *shongololo*
and it stung stung stung
as it hit her throat.

Jocelyn drank nail polish remover
for its chocolatey taste
and in Emergency
they discovered her belly
full of cigarette *stoumpies.*

Me, I had a taste
for things left on the ground:
gum stuck to the sidewalk,
chicken shit, leaves, vines
and cool stones.

But I don't remember the acrid taste
or the grit ground into my teeth,
only my mouth,
open in anticipation,
my fingers
on my tongue.

Offering

At the beach, I once saw my father, surrounded by a crowd,
put his lips over the mouth of a man lying prone on the sand.

There was something in the way he worked, quickly but precisely,
and without flourish. He could have been nailing shingles,

or measuring slabs of gyprock for our grey clapboard house
that leaned into the North Vancouver drizzle long before

we got there. As a child, it always seemed to be raining,
so that now, years later, returning to the city, it is somehow

strange to be sitting on a woman's bed in a small apartment
in a warm square of late afternoon sun. And perhaps

because of the warmth on my skin, I do not think of when
we lived in that rundown house on that street where the neighbours

wrote Nigger Go Home in jaunty chalk letters that stretched
to our lane. I do not think of my mother speaking in the kitchen

late at night of our leaving, my father forever silent,
in what I came to imagine was the thin music of shame.

Why should I? At this moment, a woman is getting ready
to step out of the bathroom wearing nothing but a silk Japanese

smoking jacket, and when she does, she will stand blinking
in the bright light, then let her robe fall away,

and in that instant her white skin will shine in the afternoon light.
At this moment, I have not yet placed my hands on her neck,

cradling it, the way my father held the man at the beach, long after
he realized his breath in those dead lungs was helping nothing

and finally, he quit. The man on the beach would never return
to the earth he was born of. And I too have quit, by leaving.

Which is why I cannot tell you, father, of my own encounter
with shame. How brown my hands look on her,

and in their stillness, how useless. This bright offering
I am unable to take, this pale one that lights up the room.

Our Kate

(after the painting "Child With
Two Adults" by Mary Pratt)

– for Mary Merikle –

Into the waiting world spilled, red and bloody,
you, newborn, and all the rest of us, still wondering
(between involuntary gasps, delight) if this
then is the right place after all. Sometimes
we are lit with an obvious flash, so photographic.
Sometimes a sudden light, filling air like water,
so quick, surrounds us: bright, thick and clear.

And then, dear Kate, some memory impels us
in that light and we cry out, all fierce and alive,
like you. Alive is what I am, again, your birth
making me so. Every last place in my hollowed
life, in inundation from that stream, is glisten,
green and bathed, illuminate as you are bathed,
in simple power and gifts and being held. I hold

you, and hold onto you, clinging to your new baby
smells: sweet milk, and soap and water, not slippery
only in my remembering hands, but also in our lives.
Dumbstruck and trembling, I am, that something
such approaching perfect sees my hand and holds,
in tiny clasps, so firm and sure, all questions, easy
only in uncertainty and ecstasy and fearless grasp.

Letter to a Husband Who's Moved Out

The kettle spits on the woodstove, into which
I have just stuffed the ragged bits of these hard months.

They spill out, burning, onto the hearth tile,
and I control them with shovel and horsehair brush,

keep them from rising too high on their own hot breath.
The sun climbs the ridge behind me, having taken

a long time to reach the west coast of America,
and dragging with it the tawny heat of desert stone.

The spade-shaped balsam leaves unearth
a fierce, remedial perfume: essential oil

of deep rock split by sun. Drunk on it,
I tell you this, in faith and out of love:

When the rank water has receded into mud
and ducks mope under evergreens, I will have

taken sun into the seedcoat of my heart and started
something I can't see, and fear the end of. Stars

will have swivelled in the Lazy Susan sky.

Snakes will lie everywhere in the paths, certain
of their speed. The herbs and grey-leaved santolina

bask, and thistles surge to meet
the dipping goldfinch. Wild grass

in the wet field will wave above my head
and muzzle the cicadas' chronic buzz.

I'll walk past the rotting alder over which
the Guernsey Cream clematis blooms, and sit

beside the pond. The questing mouths of goldfish
pock its calm like ghosts of rain.

In the thicket this overheated season has become,
finches and wrens stitch the air between the ripening

berries, the towhees rage; the hummingbirds work
their own vertical tapestry in the clearing

you've hacked out between the hawthorne and the hedge.

The Yellow Kosovo Chair

At the beginning, when she sees the chair, she is grateful.
A simple wooden chair. It is like
a chair in a child's story book, dark wood.
Painted yellow once.
No seat, but a sturdy frame, nonetheless.
The chair is in need of repair.
It would not be difficult.
She is grateful.

She would like to sit down.
She is tired.
There is a lesson here to be learned, perhaps.
She cannot quite grasp it.
She wishes she had not been late to school.
At table.
Always, her eyes hurt.
She has been studying too hard.
She would rather see nothing.
She cannot rest.
She wishes they would cover her eyes.

She sits.
She shuts her eyes.
She sits.
She hears nothing.
Behind her back.
She is grateful.
She no longer hears anything.

She nods.
Her face is swollen.
Her eyes.
Her ears.
Everything.

She is tied to the chair.
Stripped, she is tied.
Naked, she is tied to the chair.
Absolutely, she is tied.
At her wrists, she is tied.
Both wrists.
At her ankles.
Both ankles.
Behind her back.
Around her throat.
Behind.

In this chair, anything can happen.
She can be done to.
Done to.
Beyond belief.
If this were not a poem,
there would be description.
She will try to memorize the poem.
It may be important later.
Pornographia.
Clichés cram like journalistic justified italic paragraphs.
Black and white photographs, outlines in the dark.

This chair is.
Beyond the pale.
Above and beyond.
Over the top.
In and out.
A crackerjack experience.
Over and above.
Up and over.
Over and out.
Back and front.
On her back.
Face first.

Fall.
On your knees.

In this chair, she is sitting.
She can be raped.
Orally, anally, vaginally.
Even dead,
this little chair will hold her
sturdy, its back straight.
Finally, once she is dead

she will still sit, perfectly upright
in this straight back chair.
Ingenuous, the design of this simple straight back chair.
It strikes her.
Despite herself, she smiles.

In this chair, she is sitting. Quite still.
Now they are angry.
She will not look at them.
She is not listening.
They begin to shout.
She is thinking about the chair.
She hears nothing, really. Not now.
She sighs, perhaps.
What do you think, they shout.
Scream, what have you learned?
Now, what have you learned?
Now — what do you think?

House Broken

Puppy taken from its own mother
too early.
His feet are big
he will be big, give him a big name
Greek god.
He likes to hide under the coffee table and shiver.
He likes to rest his chops upon the top of Papa's walking shoes,
feet that itch to kick him
maybe.

Learn to be tough Papa says. Learn to be hard.
Guard dog for the house
but the wife
in secret
holds him like a baby in her arms and says
"God damn you dog, you better live long."

The dog will grow up
she knows.
The dog will be too big to hide
and too big for her lap.
He's a shepherd
with no sheep.
Only a porch and a leash and
a back yard to do his business in one spot.
He'll learn that.

He listens to me. He don't give me shit. He don't tell me get the hot
                                                    pepper
get the car, you smell like piss, pack my bags I'm going on a holiday
without you. With the boys
with a zoom lens for all the tits on the beach in Cuba.
I don't care about the tits, big hips those Latino girls.

This dog is going to be big, strong, perfect, good.
I chew his meat in my mouth first, then give it to him.
That way he knows
he knows who is the master.
Your Papa can pretend but I named him.
He's got my name. Not his. He's mine.
He's my dog.
And he don't give me no shit.

Fossiliferous

for Jennifer Lee and Don McKay

What/who is that outcrop?
Yellow-red ochre to salt our bones.   Mud
the toothpaste ooze of it, instep-shaped,
we wash from boots, the wheels of the baby carriage
as Kane sleeps on, fist-in-mouth,
inches above
the rush of glacial melt . . . mud
as if it could not be the colour of blood.

If I should forget myself at the river
my ears will be trilobites   their tiny bones,
my teeth axed into dirt, soft palate silting up
and silver-bound wrist, clay-clogged, its lump of
sugar, tree-lymph, sunlight, amber already turned to stone.

Shall we gather at the river where Tut is — tut, tut —
sliced, cross-sectioned, core-sampled, death
mask and petrified hail of beads and lapis between ribs?
        — headline: You *Can* Take It With You
        but it will leave you behind —
your metamorphed Timex, Dali-esque,
still bends (ten-after-two),
lop-smiling 'round your —
your nothing.

The rest is crystalline, not conglomerate:
O gone, beloved tibia, incisor, but fillings intact,
the unconscious wash and trade and metaphor of Planet
Shakespeare's lyricism, lithic witticism.

We will be old enough. We will be lost enough.
As lost as that, as gulfed, gulped, swigged,
a fulfillment of minerals, uncellular,
like Herculaneum's gutted women
topped up with limestone, dolomite:
      what a lovely brow-ridge, high cheek-stone, darling,
      you are the opposite of egg   (skull eye-hole yawns) and
      great hips, too, O Supermodels, O James Deans,
      O misplaced Me/s
      O sweet hominid, sapiens, life,
      how the earth will eat your heart out.

Reading the Map

When I say the names the places glitter into being,
Mountain, River, Lake, friends' home towns
(I could visit), the steady eyes of women who spend
August putting up fruit (I could learn something),
and where we met, your face opening into smile.
I heard that snow covered the plain, knocked lights out
so I touched your place on the map to warm you. Did you
feel it? Regarding Navarino Bay recently
I said the island's name aloud, *Sfakteria,* a squawk
and a beating of wings, and a young Athenian appeared at
arms, his bare back cross-hatched and bleeding.
He flew at his opponent in the way game birds are roused
from shrubs. I remember how his cousin whispered to me
on the bus down from Sparta, his young uncle
took me around in a black Mercedes, told
stories, how the island got its name, *slaughter, ah,*
this little shepherd's hut here in the pines on the right,
I wanted to buy it so I could gaze down the valley
as Nestor did. Money was not the problem:
the damn shepherd wouldn't sell! while all I could offer
was strawberries. At the palace gate a cat sidled up,
furred my ankle, scruffy old tom with a nose for
a picnic. Love,
                    do not be one of the hunted.
This is a most beautiful bay after a storm,
a small boat and his lady's dress half off.
Sun pouring water into a red bath.
I long for your company. Be assured —
I will walk out to meet you
                    but will I know you?

After the Walk

Swallows and swifts announce evening, the borrowed
typewriter in half-light reproaches me.
What I want to say — I have no idea.
Perhaps if I describe it: acorns, in my stomach.
Their hollow crunch on pavement.
In lawns they burn holes.
I've heard you can stew them if necessary.
Did you know that?
Maybe I'm making it up.
Walking the Roman road with you then I saw
saplings in centuries-old olive trees, the snap
and slow return of time, steady
slap of leather on rock under stocky legs
used to marching.
I wake at the darkened table with a jolt
"with this marble head in my hands" and understand
I could walk this road a hundred times
and not remember where the turn was
or why the bridge seemed cooler mid-way.

Queen Anne's Lace

I don't want to remember the summer you were seventeen
appearing on my doorstep on spindly stilt legs
a flimsy-stemmed flower, Queen Anne's Lace
teetering on the gravelly edge of some roadside
playing chicken with yourself.

I don't want to remember your hands fluttering in circles
over the fruitbowl, weighing the consequences
of eating three cherries or two strawberries
while your tongue lapped delicious memories
whipping the fury of your appetite.

I don't want to remember your anorexia
depressed on every one of us until we were crushed
by its millstone, choking on your pollen dust
of grief and anger. I wanted to forget
the summer I wished you to be eighteen,

wearied of your little whispers crumbling
on your tongue like communion wafers
washed down with sacrificial tears
because you couldn't break
a promise you made to yourself

tired of my search for life-saving words
sick of preparing recipes you swore
appealed to you on the page
but found too fat on the plate.
I wanted to shout *the kitchen is closed.*

Family Album

Although she wore it often
there is no picture of her
wearing her wide-brimmed
apricot straw in family albums.
Photographs of her are so rare
she appears an outsider,

a tourist who has lost her passport.
She was the obliging waiter
joking and capturing moments,
click, click, click,
family and friends on film
while the gravy thickens.

Photos secured with black glued corners
captioned in white ink on black matte
finally abandoned
in shoe boxes
to be used as a filing system
when she got around to it.

Visiting grandchildren
poked through the disarray
their baby selves, their
parents as children.
Snapping polaroids of a good time
was not something

her husband would do. He captured
nameless bathing hippopotami
in his telephoto lens;
boxes of wildebeests and
strangers stored
under the empty beds.

No one he has kept in touch with.

The Woman Beside the Lake is Reading

The woman beside the lake is reading
is trying to read the same page
of the same book she has been trying to read
all week
beside the same lake.

The rhythm of summer lulls her
the indolent rhythm of water
the lake with its thousand bodies
singing, dancing
below the threshold of perception
so that the mind slows
and the words on the page spin away
inconsequential
despite their freight of grief.

All summer she has been reading novels
and in novels this summer children suffer
acutely and often
and in ingenious ways.

Her heart is grey and tearful.
Her heart is a lake, its thousand bodies
dancing below the threshold of perception.

At the edge of the lake her own children play.
They are always busy. Right now
they are constructing dwellings for the creatures of the lake
involving sand and stones and blackberries
and complicated systems of irrigation.
No one has hurt them too badly yet
she thinks
unless all this building is a form of sublimation
a novel without words
depicting various forms of suffering
in ingenious ways.

The woman beside the lake is reading
has been trying to read all week

the book,
        the lake,
                the children.

A Missing Letter, or, Homesick

for Robert Kroetsch

(please insert as/if indicated)

You will pardon me for writing out of
the blue, this way

The alarm goes off at random intervals in
the coffee shop where I came to think

It is June 15th, 1995, the streetcar tracks
are being replaced

If the self is, *(quick)* silver, suggested by common sounds,
s, l, v/f — the vowel-semi-vowel a slippage

from el (health) to il (ill
The rattle of crockery, the sound of steam

And in Winnipeg it might be green as June flung up
the bole into the canopy spreading its awning over the old porch

Whereas the old perch hangs motionless under the lip of
the bank, the gold-brown light sifting (or do I mean shifting?)

In some places it is light, in some places

The missing letter blows into a corner of the ploughed field at dusk

Romeo is waiting in the portico shadowy behind a pillar, iconic,
while the daisies blow in roadside ditches

The book fell out of my hands, pages fluttering open, the letters
fled, all of them, forming a V across the eastern sky

That grid of fields tossed out by shadows,
the clouds turning over from time to time

Fear of loss, of less, that homeland. Did
you know you had dropped this?

Chac Mool

(Chichen Iza, Mexico)

We rounded a corner in the ruined city,
found the crumbling statue at our feet;
a boy pointed — *Chac Mool!* in a whisper
both gleeful and confident: barely submerged
in gesture and tone, the importance
of horror, and how it attracts.

— Then my own delight as we sighted another Chac Mool
atop a distant temple pressed against
the rainforest, that recognition: his unsupported recline,
his body in a lying-down S, knees up
and, between his hands, on his slender belly,
the empty dish awaiting the torn-out heart.
A face, as empty as the dish, turned to us,
                    asking,
                              What exactly
have you sacrificed your heart for? Whose heart
will you place in my hands, and for
what better good?

I prepare my offerings. First
I hold out my yearnings, bright-red, arterial, but
he is not satisfied, nor does he want
my sins, my sicknesses. When I lean my ear
into his crumbling face, he whispers,
it is your emptiness I want, what is left
behind after the heart is torn away.

       One after another,
the dark green one, the blue one, the many black ones,
each the weight of a metal heart,
I place in his lap my father's fourteen
motors, rust-red around their stamped labels.
My hands blacken with the thickness of old oil,
its crust and corrosion, as I haul them
from his basement, two-stroke motors,
the throb and whir silenced, the surround of grief

dense as the rainforest enclosing
the sunbaked square mile of ancient city.

What Dreams Assume

. . . I hate it when your own dreams treat you as stupid.
— Louise Gluck, "Condo"
(*American Poetry Review* 27:4)

When she was trying to convince me
to part with a small shred of my self, a tooth or
a bone in my toe, the dream assumed my integrity
and my body's wholeness. But laid bare
the incompleteness of my resolve.

Dreams assume you are multilingual,
that you can understand the body's conversations
with botany and architecture and food;
that you are familiar with fancy dress balls,
comfortable in yellow chiffon. The language of colour.
You visit country after country,
but most are called the Netherlands.
Dreams have a way with names.

The two keys, wish and fear, do not always fit
precisely into crusted old keyholes, but dreams know
who jammed the lock with a needle.
All your life you are collecting keys, looping them
on an old chain clipped to your belt.

Dreams do not value originality, especially in forms of danger:
they expect you not to laugh
at being a maiden tied to a railway track
rescued by a married man at work
who knows electricity as well as he loves you.

They assume you want to see the recently dead
smell their body scents, hear the precise timbres
of their voices, but they will withhold those pleasures until
you have stopped longing for them — then
send you a suitcase with your friend's
brown leather jacket, the label slit away from the satin lining.

They have an understanding about vases on a high shelf,
how they can change into extinct Chinese animals
with slow blinking eyes. They expect you not to hesitate
at the swimming pool's sting when its water
is replaced with soy sauce, deep,
saltier than any ocean.

Dreams recognize your expectations and failings,
assume you will encounter your fears
with equanimity, but will generously make you
as small as a turtle whose mother was a butterfly.
They assume some insects have parents of different species,
that flowers are occasionally mechanical, hiding tiny mirrors
that require adjustment, repair. Or that birds
need exercise and will devise watery contraptions
for providing it.

Dreams do not suppose that you live in this century, this body.
They do not care about your precise age,
what gender you have been reared into,
and when you are in danger, they assume your attention
is elsewhere. They suspect you need to consider
your part in your father's death. They have their own anatomy
of the foreign and the familiar.

Like poetry, dreams know more than you,
the entire field, figure, ground and foreground
and your solitariness therein.
Dreams believe there is a remedy,
they always know where to begin,
with the enlargement of the catastrophe all the way to Hiroshima.

Dreams themselves are fond of sleeping,
unaffected by your petitioning and your patience:
this casts doubt on your sincerity.
They dislike being aroused, having a net
thrown over them on waking — this is why
they are sometimes sullen and punishing,
make you cry out or gasp in terror,
or why they rebel, sitting for months by a deep volcanic lake.

Two Weak Arms

for A.B.

Two weak arms: how to be useful still,
now that I can no longer row a boat
any distance at all, carry a child
upstairs at bedtime, or even tap lightly
at the keys for very many hours.

In this weakness Rapunzel's story revisits me,
its earlier version: how later tellings
suppressed her twin sons
who fled the tower with her
into the desert, awaiting their blinded
father's return. Am I being asked now
to survive as the tale has, simplified,
the two voices muted,
and carrying less love, less truth?

Here in this boat where I pause, mid-lake with you,
caught in the lake's green net with its mirroring rim
I pull up the heavy oars, my back
to my destination: my destination is a tiny
reflection in your eyes. Straining
to what point on its circumference, this
is our discussion, while the waterbugs
stitch quick weightless arcs on the surface.

Moving will help, but so will staying still. Listen,
as I begin the story again.

The Cemetery at Vysehrad

It's quiet here, and soon it will be dark.
The living are still busy with their work,
Lighting the candles in the grave-lanterns
And making chestnut crosses on the tombs.
They plant flowers and pull out weeds. A boy
Leans a stuffed dog against a marble stone.
There is comfort in all of this, I think.

My own parents have asked to be cremated.
They told me this over Sunday dinner.
I pictured giant ovens, then the box,
Perhaps an urn, a jar with screw-top lid,
Shelved with the paperbacks in my bookcase,
Displayed for guests like knickknacks from a trip,
A trophy given to the eldest child.

Or would my brother and I have to share
The dust, dividing it up with a spoon
Like ice cream — here's for you and here's for me —
Comparing bowls to see who got the most?

Or would I scatter them someplace, unsure
Of where, what spot, the wind would let them rest?

My father argues that the dead don't care.
He says that graves are for the living — true,
He's right, but I am selfish. Let me have

This. Let me polish marble, pull the weeds,
Pick up a stray gum wrapper by your graves.
Let me leave presents, wreaths, let me pretend
That what I do is useful. Let me be
This woman, brushing dirt off her knees,
Collecting pots, old wax, some garden tools,
Her bottled water, dead plants for the trash,
Returning in the darkness to her life.

The Quiet in Vermeer

In Vermeer's paintings,
    we look through half-opened doors
        to distant rooms, anticipating
            illumination.
It's a private room we're led to
    where a woman with lute pauses
        to look out the window. So too
            woman with pitcher, woman
with pearl necklace, an astronomer
    at his table. Each   alone
        on the canvas, each drawn to the light
            moving inward.
The rooms are so quiet
    you would *not* hear a pin drop
        though you could see the light glint off that pin, ruffle
        the nap of the heavy rug, glimmer
in polished gold pitchers, the lustre of pearls,
    in glazes and glasses of plum-coloured wine.
        There are satin jackets the colour of yolk, red dresses
        like persimmons bursting.
When the woman is not alone,
    as the girl at her music,
        she looks squarely at us: *why*
        have we come?
Whose letter? Vermeer does not explain
    but we are not left in the dark. We feel the sun
        through painted window warm
        on our face.
This is the only light pure enough
    to fix such stillness, a stillness that captures
        the interrupted moment,
            moment of deep reflection

when a man, a woman gaze off
   to an inner world
      whose light is drawn
         from a different source.
And this is what Vermeer painted
   slowly, very slowly,
      in one room in a house on a busy street
         in Delft, where he lived with his wife,
his mother-in-law, his eleven children,
   collectors coming and going commissioning him,
      as he kept painting and painting
         until he died in great debt at the age of 43.

Peripeteia

All too often a cloud cover is incomplete,
leaks light at the edges, afterglow of some

conflagration of which only the birds could
have knowledge. You see them in the twilight

pecking at the plowed rows of field hardening
in frost, a dust of snow unexpectedly early.

What kind of seeds could they be picking at?
It is a lack of imagination that makes me say

it this way. I cannot stay here too long.
The sun glints in the windows of the houses.

Dylan in Duluth

After the lights go out and he's standing
behind the curtain listening to the freight-train roar
of applause, waiting to go out one last time,
he gets this whiff of sweat and piss over
the incense, another drafty hockey rink and this one
too damn close to home, and he gets to thinking
of someone — who do you suppose it might be,
Woody, maybe, old Woody and Cisco and
rambling Jack, Little Arlo maybe, or Joannie,
Joannie and Joni, maybe, or Koop and some
of the old gang he used to hang with back
in the old days in the Village — but, no, it's
the Big Bopper, Chantilly lace and a pretty face,
yeah, the old Big Bop himself, dead all these years,
bit the big one along with Holly and Ritchie Whatshisname
in a farmer's field just down the road
a ways, that road at the edge of town he'd noticed
near the airport, heading south and forever, just like
at home, all gravel and heatwaves.

                    That plane
must have really smelled of sweat and piss
in its last moments, Holly and Whatshisname
singing out a clear harmony of fright, but he imagined
the Bop was silent, stoic in the dizzying face
of his fate, either that or too blind drunk to know. Oh,
Baby. He thinks of all the planes he's been on,
all the close calls, thinks about all the lies
he's told, all the truths he's hinted at, stumbled
toward. They made a cult of Holly, scissored his likeness
out of the clear night sky and pasted it onto fridges
long past their due date, and the other guy, Ritchie, he
was another one spared the indignity of growing old

with everyone watching, forever young
in the broken corn, ribbons and bows, ribbons
and bows. But it was the Bop he'd always
liked, admired, oh, a no-talent clown, sure, but the man
had style, and he knew something most of us take
a lifetime of rock and roll to figure out. That's what
it's really all about, isn't it, a face, burning
in the third row, a face you can't ever forget, a face
caught in your throat, a scrap of lace.

Jarman Motors

Everyone I meet has your name:
grad student, janitor, coke-weary cook,
but you're across the border,
paving a bridge outside Jasper,
bunking at Pocahontas, your hands
still gripped for the scabbler.
I get $3.25 an hour at a bookstore
in Seattle, room with a German,
drink Red Hook at the Central
and, one Saturday night, pacing
the deck of the Bainbridge ferry,
lean over the stern, staring,
dramatically, at the dark spit
of the turbines, scaring my date,
although all I am doing
is counting the dollars each day
will add. Heading home after work,
up Broadway to Capitol Hill,
I nearly rear-end a Mazda,
Alberta plates, your family's name
in chrome on the trunk.
It's like dreaming about someone
who's dead; I want it to last,
following your name past the Roanoke,
over the rivets of the floating bridge
and into the strip malls of Bellevue,
not knowing or caring where I am going.

New Mother

You can smell the boredom,
fear and desperation —
how silly the fathers look
to her now, how she longs
to return to the doctor's arms,
to the bullying nurses
of the labour/delivery room.
You can smell the love
which smells like fuel oil,
like smouldering dust, like every
minute of every day spent
in futility, in walking the baby
in circles so he will sleep,
in waking the baby from sleep
so he will sleep, in feeding
and feeding and feeding
the baby — tears and exhaustion

and blood in bright clots
staining the fragrant pads
stuck between her thighs
or slipping into the toilet
like fragmented bodies, frayed
torsos and limbs, a new mother
losing it on the bathroom tiles.
When the baby stirs,

the new mother zips herself
into loose velour, soothes
the baby with a breast,
a song, a ride in the car —
the highway that passes the hospital,
searching for the window
where it happened, craving the danger,
the pulse racing, the person
she was before she became
someone she can't understand
without bleeding.

Our Father Who Art in Las Vegas

Our father who art in Las Vegas
picks his nails all day.
He's got a Cadillac, a system
for craps and a scarecrow
wife in big dark glasses
who wraps his crackers
in two layers of plastic.
He dreams of roulette,
of losing weight, of seeing
a specialist who will listen,
who will tell him exactly
what it is that is killing him.
His daughters who won't visit
love him but can't tolerate
his laboured affection, the way
he worries about them,
wishes they were men.
He dines at Excalibur's lunch
buffet where the roasted
chicken is skinned and boned
and the lettuce bleached
a pale green like sheets,
like the eyes of the girl
at the till with whom
our father smiles and purrs
as he hands her the voucher
he got from the blackjack
dealer who's fond of him,
who never had a father
like ours, who laughs
at the jokes out of Isaac
Asimov's book and takes
our father's money as gently
as he can.

Pastoral for an Urban Lover

some of them say the land resists naming
words slide off it like ice from the
escarpment into driftwood cove

city folk, all of them
ones whose wilderness is
ten feet deep along the four hundred,
animals who imagine karst
as a piece of rock

words from my country are ones you can taste
sour and crisp as macintoshes
pebble-sized
picked early when september means city
nibbled slowly in keppel township fields

i can whisper the names for you
slur the syllables and laze around the vowels
inverhuron, lion's head, dyer's bay
i hear it takes soft things to tease and
titillate the metropolitan ear

i could amuse you with parochialisms
phrases gleaned from full-time fishermen on
hunting trips north of the checkerboard
misspellings three foot high
in proud white paint on the
silos of family farms

i've ripe analogies for you
but they are bitter fruit for an urban tongue
better to spread a load of birch leaves on the floor
let you crunch across them barefoot
than to dwell upon the
slap on pavement
echoing down wellesley street

a smooth, cold kiss in a solution cave
that's how i know karst

All I Have is the Night

when I woke up this morning
the world fit me like a second skin
two metres across, one and a half down,
roughly the size of my bedroom window,
and deep enough to contain only a few
tree branches pasted to the sky;
a magpie sailed in, cleaned its wings
then just perched there, toy pterodactyl
feet of wire, stare fixed east

by the time I had finished showering
the world included a sleepy child
searching for matching socks, a street,
man walking his dog, further down
an intersection beginning to fill with cars,
an office tower, which like a fertilized egg
immediately split into two towers, four
eight, sixteen

at breakfast, the frame around the window
cracked, ripe seedpod spilling seeds of a city
all over the horizon, gates wide open, trucks
full of oranges streaming in, wheels of cheese,
fresh radishes, fresh cilantro, tons of coffee beans
from somewhere out there

the glass shattered, it was no longer quiet —
by noon what had begun as one dog barking,
flushing of toilet, quick exchange of dreams,
had grown into a hum of a hundred sewing machines,
rapidly increasing in volume, jack hammer
lathe, power drill, the pitch rising

against the background of numbers fired
into the universe at supersonic speed
rattattattattatta
hard to distinguish from bullet fire
the sofa, the paintings hanging in shreds,
the flower vase a pile of deadly slivers
all over the ruined floor

it is suppertime. I am deaf
and all but blind from the relentless flashing,
light scours my retinas in clever patterns,
faces outlined in lust, now envy, now tribal angst
forest of hands wrung in sorrow, somewhere
mindlessly clapping, stroking a cat
long gallery of stomachs, some bulging
many hollow —

        and to think,
all I have is the night to shrink it all back
to the size of my window

The Camp Fag

The Camp Fag
At Tamarack sinks
Whenever he tests.
No bright badge to sew on his Speedo
This summer.
                    He can't canoe alone.

The Camp Fag
Can't catch for shit
                    And fumbles the frisbee.
The Camp Fag, caught bed-wetting,
Is dangled over the lake
And tied to a tetherball pole.

The Camp Fag, picked last by his cabin-team,
Abandons soccer to wander
Long hours in the woods,
Kept company by his Walkman
And busy with a pocketful
Of boondoggle.

The Camp Fag stones
The turtle with no remorse,
Headphones blaring Blondie;
Pisses on the smashed shell
And laces a new bracelet by dinner.

The Camp Fag is happiest
On the bus ride home:
Hungover counsellors play cards behind.
He devours each road sign
As if it were a bread crumb.

Vati's Orange

The scent, yes,
but also the feel
of the nippled orb,
shy shine on its puckered skin:
my task, sitting at the left hand
of *Vati,* to strip off the peel,
lay bare (without tearing)
an inner flesh traversed
by whitish threads, trace
of segmentation. Then
to separate one section
from the next, running again
the risk of a tear leaking
sweet, sticky fluid
down my fingers. I was
seventeen and full
of desire
(he had me brush his hair)
to please *Vati,* fifty,
(wispy hair, soft bristled brush):
I, the chosen one,
preferred over *Mutti,* Gisela, Renate
to perform
Vati's after-dinner
Apfelsine,
the brush's caress,
these maiden rituals.

To My Mother, On the Eve of Open Heart Surgery

These last weeks, I've longed
for one more story,
something about your life
you've never told me.
just before sundown
they wash you all over, coat you
in a special solution and when
they have gone, you tell me

how your father was short
but his arms and chest and shoulders
were muscular, covered
with dark curly hair
how every night
when your father came in from the fields
he would wash
his arms and chest and shoulders
how the old sink in the kitchen
was deep and wide and looked out
on the pasture that sloped to the river
how your father would lather
his arms and chest and shoulders
then fill the dipper and rinse it all off
how then your mother would go to your father
and soap his back, lather it over and over
both of them looking out on the pasture
that sloped to the river

your eyes now on the setting sun
watching your mother washing your father's
back, her hand making the journey
over and over

Koko Loves Lips

I

If words are berries,
the mind picks them, speechless with hunger.
The inner ear digests each one
long before the voice flavours syllables
with sound.

If some words lie
beside the road, their sweetness is trampled.

If the richest patch clusters in shaded regions
of the brain, every brain
is berry-stained.

II

A San Francisco gorilla chatted
on the Internet last week. *Koko loves Lips,* she said.
Lips is Koko's codeword for *woman,*
her female handler at the zoo.

Koko is not a gorilla, she is
an experiment. Her vocabulary
of 2000 could get anyone by, even without Lips.
The secret is to pick the juiciest 2000.

Only her form of address
has changed. Still behind bars,
Koko considers her freedom
of speech a sham.

She emails Lips, but doesn't know
Lips, too, resides in a cage almost as big
as her mind.

Lips, she pleads, *Grunt eloquent.*
Berry-stain your thoughts. Pretend
you are a gorilla hunting for the 2001st word.
Go ape with me.

Baldspot

Because it is utterly open to heaven and all its blessings.

Because when consciousness escapes my body at the moment of death
no clinging tendrils will deflect its homeward flight.

Because of the seven cakras it is the crown, the thousand-petalled
rainbow-coloured lotus.

Because Don Juan told Carlos Castaneda that a warrior wears death
on his right shoulder but I wear it every day on the top of my
head.

Because while age shrinks the rest of my body, it alone continues to
grow.

Because without it I might believe I will live forever.

Because it is a beacon to our little friends from outer space, showing
them where they can safely land.

Because in seventeen tongues in seventeen lands it signifies virility.

Because it is the size and shape of a yarmulka, reminding me of all
the minyans from which I absconded.

Because it could be innocently mistaken for a tonsure.

Because I always wanted to pass for a Christian brother. As I have
always wanted to use the word tonsure in a poem.

Because I need not ask for whom the bathtub drain clogs. It clogs
for me.

Because of my hats. My green corduroy fedora whose brim I tilt
at a rakish angle when I step out for a night on the town. My
widebrimmed honest Panama for a day's digging in the garden.
My blue Rastafarian bonnet spun of the wholesome hemp. And
all the woolen watch caps that have uncomplainingly shed the
winter rains.

Because through it my body is attuned to Gaia, and I grieve for her
losses even as I grieve each falling hair.

Because it waxes with the ozone hole of Antarctica and wanes with the
coastal forests of B.C.

Because it is both map and memory, keeping score of my wanderings
like the rings of an ancient tree.

Because even as desert spreads through Africa's grasslands, it devours my remaining cover.

Because it provides me daily practice in renunciation, and prods me to incremental progress in the arduous spiritual discipline of letting go.

Because its presence is that of absence and thus inclines me to the metaphysical.

Because it removes all impediments and interference, releasing me to write without restraint off the top of my head.

The Used Car Salesman's Fantasia

Don't browbeat me with talk about quotas.
Let's give up all thought of selling Toyotas,
Dodges, Pintos, Falcons, Fords in the Dakotas.

I want a slower means of locomotion
than the ones at Earl's First Choice Auto.

I want a dancing girl with castanets,
not a customer kicking some car's tires
and asking me to throw in cleated radials,

while Earl plays golf and chats with bankers,
leaving Lloyd and me to sell his klunkers.

I want a palanquin with an ostrich-feather fan
and four retractable handles, so I can be
hoisted like an Assyrian satrap

and carried for miles along high dunes
within sight of the Indian ocean.

But before I start issuing edicts, make sure
my bearers receive the corporate rate.
I want them all to have beach cabanas

and eight weeks' paid vacation,
free health care and hot-day replacements —

people who'll carry me slower
when the simoom or the khamsin blows
and I still get the urge to see the ocean.

That's for you, Earl, of the signet ring,
diamond cufflinks and pompadour.

Don't float rumours about cutting staff,
or cry about dwindling customer care.
Just get me a light-weight travelling chair

and someone to beat out time on a drum
as we follow the undulant line of the dunes.

An Evening with You in Vancouver

I inhale the wind's chilled bouquet
of fresh earth and crisp cotton

as a blanket of dusk slips
off my thighs.

Funny how it's longing that keeps me still
listening for your voice on the back porch.

But my neighbour cordially
refuses to be silent,
and Blue snores like an accordion at my feet
and the grass grows a painful green
and the orchestra of family dinners
erupts from kitchen windows.

There are moments when I am beside myself
with missing you,

when my body relinquishes
the chair it sits in and the night it waits for
just to witness my love
                                    unfolding.

Do you ever feel that?

When you pour a glass of water at the kitchen table
or wake to a rainstorm in the middle of the night
or sort through a basket full of warm laundry.

When I sit on the back porch at twilight

unable to tear my eyes away from a curtain of clouds
as the sky changes into the colour of yearning,

some simple moment in my life
disrobes, to hold you
                    closer.

A Story

for Jennie Thomas

Be patient and words will come.
Language, like a flock of sparrows lifting itself
right through the ceiling,
has left the whole group. Some
are weeping and the woman
who has just told us the story of her son,
the brilliant-eyed child who would stand on the bed
with his arms outstretched for a hug,
the one who, when she finally came to him,
would leap and draw her to him
collapsing her with the weight
of his love, this woman stands
with her hands clasped in front of her
as if they were aware of the emptiness
so often between them.
The child died.
It is up to me to break the silence
but there are no words in the cave of my mouth.
A small animal has burrowed
into the hollow of my throat
and nothing, at any rate, should be set free
to roam the thick, textured place between us
that connects us without language,
not a single syllable will pounce into the room's silence
to perform in the feathered air.

What We Don't Think of Packing

but take along anyway: the shoes on our feet,
the fifty-four bones in our hands, the memory of
the colour of the sheets on our beds. We prepare
for flight as if we and the customs officers are the only

ones who will ever open our baggage. Nightshirts close
to the suitcase's zipper so when we arrive we can quickly
begin to restore what we thought we'd lost. Certain kinds
of loss we bargain for in transit: eight hours of sleep,
the memory of where we parked the car —

In Canada a man stands at the end
of his driveway talking to a neighbour: *I received*
the call — search and rescue. There was no screaming, no
arms hanging loose. The helicopter shone light on the water
and we picked up what there was —

When I walk the beach with the kids
I know what I'm looking for.
I found a piece of plane and put it in my pocket.
Didn't tell the kids — a scrap
the size of a two dollar coin.

Loss jangling, except that it's in a currency
no one else understands even if they were on the boat
when he cupped the child's sneaker in his palm, insisted
the police promise to return it to the family — We never

anticipate losing the memories of what we have already lost —

Van Gogh Dancing

I had lunch with Van Gogh yesterday
and he told me what he'd been doing
all these years in the afterlife and
I told him about the incredible egg rolls in the
Chinese restaurant we were sitting in and
he told me about death and transcendence
and the limits of earthly knowledge
but all I could think about was whether
I should buy Macintosh or Granny Smith apples
at the grocery store and which would
sit better with egg rolls and then I looked
at the artist sitting across from me and
wondered that he hadn't aged and
thoughts of cheese and wine and other things that taste better with age
flooded me and then it started raining and Vincent got very excited
because he hadn't felt rain for some time
because there is no rain in the afterlife and
I wasn't at all surprised to see him jump out of his chair and
run outside twirling in the rain like a petite French
ballerina and I thought if I were
an artist myself that would be my painting
(Van Gogh Dancing in the Rain Circa 1998)
and the art world would never understand that the moment was real
and the only other witness would be Mr. Wong
but he was sick yesterday and couldn't tell Vincent from an elephant —
and I feel bad because our egg rolls
are getting cold but I don't want
to ruin the rainy moment for Vincent though he might not
even know the difference between hot or cold

egg rolls anyway and he's probably wishing for cornbread
or nineteenth-century French wine while he's outside
spinning gracefully and all I can offer
is Mr. Wong's egg rolls cold and when he
finally comes inside I ask him to tell me more about
art and mortality thinking he'll be interested
but all he wants to talk about is how much he missed the rain . . .

Small

We are sliding on the ice,
my husband saying he can't
stop, headlights coming closer
until death is a little scarf
pulled through my ears
by magic
the brakes catch on something
and the truck whistles
past. Our small

lives given back to us
for the moment
as we imagine wreckage,
parts of the car in the snowy
ditch, limbs askew, things
scattered everywhere: what
might have been.

Think of anything but this,
maybe an insect
turned upside down on a table,
tiny legs bicycling
against air, until something rights it,
lets it go
wherever it wants: into the garden
or back in the glass jar.

July 15, 1887

The engineer sees the freight train
far off, on the St. Thomas crossing
and tries reversing — forehead slick,
belly tight — when the air brakes don't
work. The fireman scrambles up,
pulling the brake on the baggage car,
and now the engineer reads
Michigan Central Railway
painted yellow on the cars
filled with oil,
while evening glazes the plate
glass windows on Talbot street,
stretches itself over the low fields,
lingers in these seconds, time elongated
into something about to happen,
as the blue shadows of the passing cars
race over the ground, over
the fireman who has jumped
from the train, skinning his knees as he tumbles,
rolling into the ditch and covering
his ears.

The explosion — so loud
it echoes from that century
to this — breaks the plate glass windows,
shudders the houses, sweeps fire
through the cars like brooms
so that no one has
half a chance, even the man
from the livery stables trying to douse
the flames on the roof
until he's caught, licked golden
as a god
against a sky gone black with smoke.
He stands on the shingles, arms outstretched,
poised to fly.

Rain Presses Gull

We think we remember the sun once on cedar chairs
Lavender on the wind and lazy docks calling.

But memory is selfish in rain like this.
A dozen men with tiny hands holding only me.

This storm is so perfect it's like skinny dipping at Sylvan Glen
Past midnight with all the Bartney boys, even little Frank.

The bed's tired from wave after wave of rain
In East Sooke, the grass lepers in my hands at low tide.

November rain presses gull under the boat overturned for winter's
                                                            wait
When the sun's still drunk, sings Leonard Cohen way past noon.

The spare room weeps when the rain stays this long.
Rain has no manners, slaps the side of the house,

The way Uncle Finnegan expected dinner always at five.
In this rain my husband can't undress the river running through us.

This rain is an honest woman out of place
A superstitious feast of high heels and lampshade.

The red-winged bird is back; we hear the flight
Speaking in riddles, says anyone can have more than two hands.

I wear November rain under my dress, slide onto a desk.
For a moment we have outwitted storm, let go the bird.

I blow bubbles through a flat straw until the cup overflows.
Rain's such a flirt. Presses me down, and down, down.

Adam Naming the Animals

He brought them to the man to see what he would
call them, and whatever he called each living creature,
that was its name. Genesis 2:19

I

At first, of course, he did not understand.

Speechless, clay between his fingers,
he wandered into the trees
where creatures darted and burrowed.

You must name them, the voice urged.

The man gestured to each animal,
saw their differences flickering in the shade.

But the voice said, name them.

He gathered blossoms to wreathe their nests,
made piles of rocks where they had stood,

but still the voice said, name them.

The man feeling something
like a blade within him, shouted: "I cannot."

Good, said the voice, now name them.

II

They would not fit inside the words.

Sounds bolted shut in his mouth.
Ohs fell from his throat.

His tongue, feeling its corners,
searched under itself for explanations.

He wanted words with barbs —
something to still them:

they squirmed and flashed in the leaves,
clicking, he thought,

like bones hung in the branches.

III

He learned to see time
outlined in yellow on the slopes and burning
at the edges of his hands.

Kneeling on a rain-soaked log,
he saw a print and bent
to touch its four flanges blooming in the mud.

"This is who I am", he said and followed
the tracks to a cave,
where the air had been swallowed

in a cold stench. He'd seen the cave,
heard at night the padding of its thoughts
leaving its mouth, seen the shapes

of these sounds. He wandered
towards its dark pout,
"this is who I am", he said, entering.

Silence brushed his legs. In this absence
of sight, he waited
for the cold depth of vowels.

IV

The voice returned and found the man
shivering near a creek,
knots of sound coughing from his throat.

It clothed him with a hush,
asking: "would you rather be water, perhaps stone,
something carried lightly by wind?"

The man folded his words
back in his lungs, breathing:
"make me music, a song hurtling from the bush."

The voice was silent.

In the woods, with a sound like rain,
the animals leapt away.

Moon Above the Ruins

There is only the moon
        above
the ruins of Tashme.

Takeo came out
of his internment cabin
playing his *shakuhachi*
a mournful tune
      blowing dry through the bamboo
      tunnel of that instrument

minor notes bent to the wind
rose to the parched, mad moon
during that early august

one by one
the other prisoners
emerged
into the dry light
looking for the sun
that was never
to rise again
        we sought
the warmth of each other
     we knew that time
was over
        one by one
we left the camp
and ventured in-
to the cool mountain
breezes
that came down and blew
through our shrinking selves

arid cracked voices   drew
together and rode
bareback
on the hollow notes
of that old flute
until the rock mountain faces
          sang back to us
an ancient pentatonic
song

there is only the moon
since the august sun
exploded over hiroshima
          burning paper cranes
and freezing shadows
          during the cusp of sunrise
and moonset.

hisashi goromaru
1910–1987
Tashme, B.C.
1945

Note: Terry Watada's poem appeared in *Vintage 97–98*, but with some lines missing. The League apologizes for this error and is pleased to be able to re-publish the poem — this time in its entirety.

In the Beginning

The cats slept in the woodshed.
Before the sun rose, they'd climb the fire escape,
paws shuddering the thin ladder of morning.
Their cries woke the dead but they could not wake me.
While my husband was gone
I dug up the ground and planted a garden.
It failed as things often do.
What with the soil, what with the deer.
I'd sit on the roof and listen to his shirts snap in the wind.
Or lie in three inches of bath water
watching my skin turn the colour of tobacco.
For my nineteenth birthday he gave me a suede belt
from which metal leaves dangled.
It was August and the creek below the house
still bubbled a kind of dark joy. I thought
a wife was someone who read a book
of recipes, then followed each one
to the end of the road. But the road turned dusty.
It grew quiet as my brain.
Some of us can't say why the bread doesn't rise —
the flour's too heavy, the yeast's too old? —
but when the fever passes,
we tie back our hair and scrub down the walls.
Each morning before leaving for work
he'd kiss me while I slept, his metal-toed boots
stepping through the tail-end of dawn.
I'd think about this on the long afternoons
I walked through the forest, understanding nothing,
wanting nothing, having nothing else to do
but move among the trees, the leaves
around my waist
like a string of silver chimes.

Smelter Town

On Friday afternoons the wooden sidewalks ran into the Skeena River.
It was no joke. We were pear trees struggling to bloom in snow.
There was a garden party once, our mother
in a short green jacket, my sisters and I gobbling
dainty ham sandwiches. Though it was lonely
eating under the kitchen table,
the thin singing
of a mosquito trapped in my ear.

Face to face with my sisters' scabbed knees
and my mother's old slippers,
I couldn't think —
what herb had been left out of the soup?

And yes
it's odd that people behave so badly toward their own children.
It's why the animals went into the forest and never looked back.

There goes my father with his cowlick bangs.
Forty years have passed since he worked in the smelter.
What more can I tell you about that aluminum town?
That all the streets were named Pheasant or Partridge or Swan?
That one summer night my mother lay
spread-eagle out on the driveway
so my father couldn't leave?

My sister also lay down and closed her eyes.
She must have been six when she said with conviction,
I know who I am,
her words drawing me up to the top bunk
where I sat on her stomach and pried her lids open.
Who, who? I demanded,
hooting
like a terrible bird.

Grip

At a stoplight
the biker's leathered hands flex
and unflex
like two greyhounds
about to eat up a track.

They are restless and insatiate
consuming what they hold
throttle
clutch
the steel bars themselves
doing what a million years of evolution
has shaped them to do with a spear
the bow of a violin.

Grip is what we lost when the cord was cut
what we look for afterwards
even as fathers
testing the strength of our new children
how long they will cling
to an outstretched index finger
not as cruel as the Spartans
who challenged their boys to stay aloft and live
or let go and die
but an examination nonetheless
the first in a long series of handshakes and arm wrestles
because the true winners of this world
are neither the most intelligent
nor the wealthiest
but those who can hang on the longest.

Grip is also a memory I have of my own father
in his last days
a man who knew he was slipping
how he took comfort in the Volvo I drove back then
embracing its overbuilt passenger handle
as though it were a stair railing or the kind of reinforced pipe
a trucker uses to climb into his cab
strong enough to console a man at the end of his life
the way my father took consolation
in both hands
gratefully
like someone who'd been in the water a long long time
terrified of going under.

What the Phone Said

Your daughter is barefoot and running.

All the chestnut trees on Cook Street cannot catch her swift heels
when she's looking for her mother.

It said rice is popping in the pantry.

The shower is melting like wax, the wine is boiling.
The ants have buried themselves deep under the back stairs.

It said forget the pencils, forget the books.
Forget the tigers burning bright.

Even the foxtrot cannot take the heat. After so many years,
Ella's stopped singing.

It said the basement is a well of broken junk.
The neighbours are gathering the dark in their arms.

Come home, it said.
Your cooking days are over, the recipes have all been lost.

It said the guitar needs cleaning, the pool table has no pockets.
The tray you bought for a dollar in the village
has carried its last cup and saucer, its last plate of brownies.

It said the kitchen is moving up and the strawberry jam
is going for a ride. Somebody left the crock out.

It said men and their toolbelts are waltzing in the foyer.
They are giving up cigarettes and letting girls
do the ladder work.

It said all the soap and all the water,
all the paint and varnish.

Your son is chasing birds, it said,
and when he runs across the gymnasium,
your words seem small.

Three Bats

I

On LSD
surrounded by nuns
in the kitchen of a convent
overlooking a golf course
I catch one
between the two halves
of a pillow folded
for that very purpose.

But I lack faith
doubt myself
in the moment of victory

Like Lot's wife
or better still Orpheus
I look back
not behind me to Sodom
or down to Hades
but into my pillow
open it inch by inch
until white cotton gives way
to eyes teeth tongue
the nuns in attendance
giggling when once again
a winged devil
flutters into the bright air
above them.

II

In 1974
echolocation
a term coined thirty years earlier
is not yet common parlance
not the word I use
only three days married
to describe
what the bat is doing
each time I throw a rock
into the dimming sky
above the lake.

Radar I say instead
admiring the animal's ability
to avoid collision
to see
what others cannot
the very word
I will use later
when a friend asks me
how I knew
something was
going on.

III

Riddle: what is splashing
underneath the bed?
Answer: you look.

At first
the bat is comic
the way an eagle is
when it tackles a salmon
too big to carry
talons groping for land
forced to swim
use its glorious wings
as paddles.

Comic then sad
how this wonder of the night
could misjudge so badly
settle in a chamber pot.

Outside
I feel like God
bailing man out again
the arrogant little bastard.

The Canadian
Youth Competition

SENIOR DIVISION

Introduction to the Senior Division

Judges: Patricia Young and Jay Ruzesky

The news today was full of reports of the high school massacre near Denver, Colorado — kids shooting kids. The discussions about the motivation for the attack have made me think back to those tough and anxious times that were my adolescence: the blazing self-doubt, the debilitating fear of not fitting in.

At the same time, I've been reading through some of the 1,800 poems submitted for the League of Canadian Poets Youth Contest, Senior category. How fortunate that poetry can also be an outlet for emotions. One of the commonalities in all of these poems is the heartfelt anguish of being young at the end of the twentieth century. It brought back a rush of agony and, honestly, despite the various trials of adulthood, it was a relief to realize that the youthful preoccupations of so many of these poems had been, in our own memories, filed away to be recollected only in the relative tranquillity of middle age.

As deeply as we were touched by the honesty and frankness of so many of these young writers, the poems that stood out for us were the ones that combined the authenticity of experience with the real craft of writing — those by poets who would take subjects like love and family and anger, and could breathe life into them and bring them closer to the experience of others by using fresh language and sharp, clear imagery. In the end, sincerity is only a part of the art of writing.

The winning poems stand up, not as good writing by young people, but as good writing period. They are poems that could have been chosen as winners in any poetry contest. Congratulations to those writers and to the ones who received an honourable mention. We look forward to reading more of you in the future. To all of the 1,797 writers who didn't grab the ring this time, we wish you good luck in the future. Keep reading and keep writing.

— Patricia Young, Jay Ruzesky

The Canadian Youth Competition
Senior Division Prize Winners

FIRST PRIZE
Jessie Carson
"Space Between Our Fingers"

SECOND PRIZE
Julia Thompson
"Pomegranates"

THIRD PRIZE
Ami Drummond
"Corn Nuts on the Back Seat"

HONOURABLE MENTIONS
Alee Chapmen, Victoria, BC, "He Is Always on Top"
Michael Cope, Invermere, BC, "A Drink with Destiny"
Adrienne Ho, Ottawa, Ontario, "I Hope It Never Comes to This"
Courtney Myette, Victoria, BC, "The Mating Dance"
Tanya Reimer, Victoria, BC, "These Scraps"
Phoebe Wang, Ottwa, Ontario, "The Two Sides of Drowning"
Liz Windhorst, Stoney Creek, Ontario, "Lanky"

Space Between our Fingers

When Mother
finds my brother under the porch
that day
she says five words
we'll never forget
"I love you this much"
Smiling, she holds her hand out
space between her fingers
not more than two inches

My mother loves his eyelashes
long like whispers
When he was younger
I
told him he couldn't play   boy baseball
because he was too pretty

From the age my brother could walk
we have wrestled
bear cubs
on our Persian rug
and I remember
always holding back
five years older was way too strong
But now   he is
bigger and when we fight
I cannot bruise him
instead
only print my nails on his arms
scattered animal tracks left in snow

And when I come home
tempered by small experience
spitting at those daring
to cross my path
my brother stands at our kitchen counter
announcing
I love my sister this much
space between his fingers
not more than two inches.

Pomegranates

That evening
the sun
set like a bloody
pomegranate
its meat
punctured
by your sharp nails
you were so eager
to eat
to sink your teeth
into flesh
I told you
eat only the seeds
the heart
of the fruit
you were so glad to kill it
staining your lips
with its red juice
but sweetness
has a weight
too heavy
for boys like you
to carry
so you let the sun drown
in its own blood
belly up
for the flies.

Corn Nuts on the Backseat

Let's just sit and crunch on corn nuts, let the salt fill your mouth and coat your fingers. Let it wrinkle your lips, drawing out their moisture. Let's just drive towards the sun until it goes down, then turn around and wait for it to come up again. Let's count cacti tonight, see how many have begun to flower, and how many will soon die. Let's just watch the woman walk her dog. Dragging him behind her, making her slow pace seem fast; like a tornado whipping through a small town or my best friend's mother whizzing through *Reitmans*. Let's just relax and wait for the corn nuts to dissolve in our mouths, to make small shaped lumps of pulp. Let's just watch *Benny and Joon* one more time, late at night with popsicles, and dill pickles, close at hand.

The Canadian
Youth Competition

JUNIOR DIVISION

Introduction to the Junior Division

Judges: Mark Cochrane and Susan McCaslin

The entries to this year's Canadian Youth Poetry Competition, Junior Category, exhibited a great range of themes and formal approaches, and a surprising level of psychological and technical sophistication for students in this age group. Poems ranged in form from the haiku, tanka, cinquain and sonnet, through the short free-verse lyric, to longer narrative poems. Entrants wrote of natural beauty, of social ills, war, and environmental concerns, of relationships and family, of body and gender.

Students at this level demonstrate a remarkable facility in the fusion of form and content. Their insights are often fresh and vigorous, marked by precocity, humour, and empathy for the disenfranchised. Portraits of animals and mythic creatures, sunsets and storms, arrived alongside poems of personal tragedy and loss, childhood's end and the critical observance of adulthood rituals from an ever narrowing distance. We were inspired and delighted by the work of these young writers.

— Mark Cochrane
and Susan McCaslin

The Canadian Youth Competition
Junior Division Prize Winners

FIRST PRIZE
Fabienne Calvert-Filteau
"Four Ways to Look at Nai Nai's Growth Chart"

SECOND PRIZE
Anne Gaspar
"A Tree"

THIRD PRIZE
Marena Winstanley
"The Politics of the School: Utensils"

HONOURABLE MENTIONS
Bronwyn Bjorkman, Vancouver, BC, "Mirrored"
Lucy Erickson, Surrey, BC, "The Lioness"
Le Zhang, Westmount, Quebec, "Maples"

Four Ways to Look at Nai Nai's Growth Chart

1. It's 1921
Margaret and Helen stand
with their backs
pressed against the wall.
Helen's feet inch upwards.
This way she is the same height
as her older sister.
The first measurements are made.

2. Margaret, Helen, Mary —
wet feet sweep across the porch floor.
Dad has insisted on measuring them
before Margaret leaves for Europe.
She is six feet tall
and when Helen stretches up on her toes
she still isn't tall enough
to reach her sister's mark.

3. Mary doesn't want to be measured.
She says that the huge belly
makes her seem shorter
and she's already short enough.
She tells Dad
that he can measure the baby instead
when it arrives.

4. Nai Nai gets a pencil
and tells me to stand up against the wall
feet flat, chin up,
I follow her instructions.
She no longer reaches the six foot mark
old age has compressed her.
She draws the line — 5'4"
and writes my name beside it.
You'll be the next to reach my mark, she says
Just wait and see.

A Tree

Dawning it is merely a cell, a runty egg.
It splits below its glowing blankets.
Cautiously bursts a puny stem.
Reaching from the soil, a quivering arm
To pull itself up.
To grasp the brisk heavens
The tree evolves muscles
And toes under covers, clutching the soil.
The legs parked durably.
Arms shoot and hands and fingers straining from the peak.

The nails are dyed vivid colours
Tumble down to the earth
The tree waves in the blow
Branches flying.
The sweet birds no longer visit.
Then its beauty is masked in whiteness
The sky rains,
Then the tree
A faint sign of life remains,
Under the skin
Flow the veins
And stem a new beginning.

The Politics of the School: Utensils

Each utensil has a distinct personality.
And its role in the realm
That is the school is outlined from its creation.

The scissors play the double role
Of rebel and psychiatrist.
Cutting and mangling,
Relieving their wielder of frustrations.

The pen is the hypocrite.
Strong and hardy on the outside
Yet all liquid on the inside.

The pencil is indecisive.
Ever conscious it leaves room for mistakes
Striving to be loved by all
Yet constantly being broken.

The eraser is the homemaker.
Always there to clean up
Everyone's mess with a beaming, if rubbery, face.

The calculator is the downtrodden one.
Slaving away
Being poked and prodded
Day in and day out
Life is no fun when you're always right
And know everything.

JUDITH ADLER lives with her son Antony in St. John's, Newfoundland. She teaches sociology at Memorial University. Her first short story, "The Road to Abu Simbel", is soon to appear in *Prairie Fire*.

BERT ALMON was born during a hurricane in Port Arthur, Texas, in 1943. His life has been relatively quiet ever since. He came to Canada in 1968 and is now a Canadian citizen. He teaches modern poetry and creative writing at the University of Alberta.

ANTONIA BANYARD emigrated from Zambia with her family in 1974. Since completing her B.A. in creative writing from the University of Victoria, she has worked in the publishing industry. She lives in Vancouver and is a member of the Seven Sisters Writing Group.

SHANE BOOK was awarded *The New York Times* Fellowship in Poetry from New York University in 1998. He has work forthcoming in *Rattle* and the *Prose Poem* in the U.S., and *The Malahat Review, Pottersfield Portfolio* and *Geist* in Canada. He is the winner of the 1999 Charles Johnson Award in Poetry in the U.S., as well as this year's *Malahat Review* Long Poem Prize.

DIANA BREBNER was born in Kingston, Ontario. She is a graduate of the University of Ottawa, where she studied philosophy, and now lives in Ottawa.

FABIENNE CALVERT-FILTEAU is fourteen years old. She lives in Ottawa and is currently in the Literary Arts programme at Canterbury High School.

JESSIE HANNAH CARSON was born and raised in Victoria, B.C., where she is currently attending her final year at Claremont Secondary. After graduation, she plans to further her education at the University of Victoria. She would like to thank her English teachers, the Stensons, for both guiding her to the freedom of poetry and sharing their love of writing.

MARLENE COOKSHAW's most recent collection is *Double Somersaults* (Brick Books, 1999). Earlier this year a poem of hers won *Fiddlehead*'s first Ralph Gustafson prize. She lives on Pender island, B.C., and is acting editor of the *Malahat Review* in Victoria.

AMI DRUMMOND has been published in the *Claremont Review* and looks forward to attending Camosun College in the fall of 1999.

CATHY FORD was born in Lloydminster, Saskatchewan, and grew up in northern British Columbia. She has a B.F.A. and an M.F.A. from the University of British Columbia (1978). She now lives on Mayne Island, and in Sidney, B.C., working as poet and fictioniste, publisher, editor, and teacher.

LUCIA FRANKA is a member of the Playwrights Union of Canada and has had twelve of her plays produced professionally, including *Joy Tide, Holy Mo, Christmas on the Air, Chickens* and *Mistletoads*. She is the playwright in residence for Chemainus Theatre in Vancouver. She has been granted a B.C. Arts Council Award, a few Jessie Nominations and a Gordon Armstrong Playwrights Award.

The title story from BERNICE FRIESEN's first book *The Seasons are Horses* (Thistledown Press) won the Vicky Metcalf Award for short story. Her "ferocious feminist verse" has recently come out in book form — *Sex, Death and Naked Men* (Coteau Books). This is her second appearance in a *Vintage* anthology.

ANNE GASPAR lives in Windsor, Ontario. She is twelve years old and is in 7th grade at a French Immersion school. She enjoys creative writing, power tumbling, ballet and cross-country running.

SUSAN GILLIS has published poetry in various Canadian literary journals and in the chapbook *Attar of Rose*. She lives in Montreal most of the time.

ELIZABETH GLENNY won the first prize and honourable mention in the Canadian Authors Association Niagara Branch Poetry Contest in

1996, and the first prize for body of work in the same competition in 1998. She has been writing poetry for several years for friends and fun.

SUSAN GLICKMAN is the author of *Complicity, The Power to Move, Henry Moore's Sheep, Hide and Seek,* and *The Picturesque and the Sublime: A Poetics of the Canadian Landscape.*

MAUREEN SCOTT HARRIS was born in Prince Rupert, British Columbia in 1943, grew up in Winnipeg, and moved to Toronto in 1964. She has a B.A. and B.L.S. from the University of Toronto. She worked as a librarian for many years. Now she is a part-time bookstore clerk, editor and writer.

MAUREEN HYNES lives in Toronto and is a faculty member at a community college. She has written ESL texts and academic manuals, and has trained teachers in China and Cuba.

SARAH LABARGE has an Honours B.A. in Creative Writing from Northwestern University. Her play *Corday* was workshopped at the Tarragon Theatre in October 1998.

CAROLE GLASSER LANGILLE, originally from New York, now lives in Lunenburg, Nova Scotia. Her most recent book of poetry, *In Cannon Cave,* was nominated for the Governor General's Award for Poetry and the Atlantic Poetry Prize.

ROSS LECKIE, a writer, editor and teacher, was born and raised in Montreal. He received a B.A. from McGill University in 1975, an M.A. in Creative Writing from Concordia University in 1982, and a Ph.D. in Literature from University of Toronto in 1990, where he studied the poetry of Wallace Stevens.. He is currently Director of Creative Writing at the University of New Brunswick and Editor of *The Fiddlehead.*

BRENT MACLAINE teaches English at the University of Prince Edward Island. He has published poetry in *The Fiddlehead, The Antigonish Review,* and *The Cormorant.* He is also a past winner of P.E.I.'s annual Milton Acorn Award Poetry Contest.

DAVE MARGOSHES grew up in the U.S., but has lived in Canada for more than twenty-five years. He attended Middlebury College in Vermont, and the University of Iowa, where he received a B.A. and an M.F.A. He works as a jack-of-all-trades: freelance writing, editing, teaching, and writing fiction and poetry. He is involved with Writers in Electronic Residence and, in 1995-96, was writer in residence in Winnipeg.

SHARON MCCARTNEY has an M.F.A. in poetry from the Iowa Writers Workshop. Her book of poetry *Under the Abdominal Wall* is forthcoming from Anvil Press.

ROBERT MCGILL has just finished an English Literature degree at Queen's University and will be beginning his Master's degree at Oxford University as a Rhodes Scholar in fall 1999.

ANNA MIODUCHOWSKA's poetry, stories, essays and book reviews have appeared in various periodicals and newspapers including *The Fiddlehead, Dandelion, Prairie Fire, Room of One's Own, CV2, Other Voices, The Globe and Mail, Edmonton Journal*, as well as in anthologies, and on the CBC Radio. *Some Flowers do Well in Flowerpots*, a poetry chapbook, was published in 1997, by Empress. *In-Between Season*, a full collection, was published in 1998, by Rowan Books.

MORLEY NIRENBERG is a Toronto-based writer and television producer. He was previously published in *Vintage '90*. In 1995 he received an Honourable Mention in the *Books in Canada* Student Writing Competition. He has just completed his first collection of poems, *Nobody Knew*.

RUTH ROACH PIERSON teaches women's history and feminist studies at the Ontario Institute for Studies in Education, University of Toronto. Her poetry has been previously published in *Canadian Forum, Contemporary Verse 2, Grain, Intersections 94*, the *People's Poetry Letter, PRISM, Room of One's Own*, and *Not to Rest in Silence: A Celebration of People's Poetry*, edited by Ted Plantos.

MARILYN GEAR PILLING lives in Hamilton, Ontario. She is the author of *My Nose is Gherkin Pickle Gone Wrong* (short fiction, Cormorant Books), and her poetry manuscript *Henhouse Longing* is currently looking for a publisher.

LORRANE RABOUD-REECE began publishing poetry intensively in 1997. This is her first publication. She is a visual artist. Currently she sells computers from a garage-based business in Bragg Creek, Alberta.

MURRAY REISS lives on Salt Spring Island with his wife Karen, a ceramic artist. His poems have also appeared, as runners up, in the '96, and *'97/98 Vintage* anthologies. His first book is tentatively called *Always a Bridesmaid.*

PETER RICHARDSON was born in Norwalk, Connecticut in 1948. Since 1977, he has been employed by Air Canada as a ramp worker in Montreal. His poems have appeared in a number of magazines including *Poetry* (Chicago), *Queen's Quarterly* and *The Malahat Review.* His first collection, *A Tinker's Picnic,* is due out in October, 1999 from Véhicule Press.

SUZANNE ROBERTSON's poems have appeared in the anthology *A Room at the Heart of Things,* published by Véhicule Press. She lives in Toronto.

JAY RUZESKY was born in Edmonton, Alberta in 1965 and now lives in Victoria. He is on the editorial board of *The Malahat Review* and is co-founder of Outlaw Editions. He has taught at the University of Victoria and, since 1990, at Malaspina University College in Duncan, British Columbia.

ELEONORE SCHÖNMAIER is the author of *Treading Fast Rivers* (Carleton University Press, 1999). She lives in Ketch Harbour, Nova Scotia.

ADAM ELLIOTT SEGAL has had several poems published in *Afterthoughts.* He is currently entering his fourth year at the University of Western Ontario where he is completing a combined English and Comparative Literature Honours degree.

ANNE SIMPSON is a writer and artist living in Antigonish, Nova Scotia. In 1997, she shared the Journey Prize with Garbriella Goliger for her short story "Dreaming Snow", first published in the *Fiddlehead*.

SUSAN STENSON teaches in Victoria. She also co-edits *The Claremont Review*, a literary venue that showcases young, emerging writers. Her work is featured in *Vintage 97/98*.

JULIA THOMPSON has been published in the spring and fall editions of the 1999 *Claremont Review*.

PAUL TYLER is from Vancouver Island and currently lives in Baltimore, Maryland where he's been working for the past two years. His poems have most recently appeared in *Event* and *Prairie Fire*.

TERRY WATADA is a Toronto writer. His credits include *Seeing the Invisible, Daruma Days* and *Bukkyo Tozen: A History of Jodo Shinshu Buddhism in Canada*. His first book of poetry, *A Thousand Homes*, was shortlisted for the Gerald Lampert Award. Along with fellow musicians Kuan Foo and Sean Gunn, he will soon release a CD of original music entitled "Hockeynight in Chinatown."

MARENA WINSTANLEY, a grade 9 student at University Hill Secondary in Vancouver, B.C., has been writing poetry since her early childhood. However, no one has ever got to see her work because it was never "good enough". This year, for the first time her poetry began to reach her expectations.

PATRICIA YOUNG was born in Victoria, British Columbia, where she now lives. Her most recent book *What I Remember from My Time on Earth* (House of Anansi Press, 1997) won the Dorothy Livesay Poetry Prize.

TERRENCE YOUNG teaches English and writing to high school students in Victoria, B.C. and co-edits *The Claremont Review*. His fiction and poetry have appeared in journals and magazines across Canada.

1988 1st poem: Michael Redhill
      2nd poem: Sharon Thesen
      3rd poem: Cornelia Hoogland

1989 1st poem: Elisabeth Harvor
          tied: Elyse Yates St. George
          tied: Patricia Young

1990 1st poem: Diana Brebner
      2nd poem: Blaine Marchand
      3rd poem: D.J. Eastwood

1991 1st poem: Elisabeth Harvor
      2nd poem: David Margoshes
      3rd poem: Debbie Fersht

1992 1st poem: Nadine McInnis
      2nd poem: Stan Rogal
      3rd poem: Louise B. Halfe

1993 1st poem: Joy Kirstin
      2nd poem: Patricia Young
      3rd poem: Gabrielle Guenther

1994 1st poem: Tim Bowling
      2nd poem: John Pass
      3rd poem: Sue McLeod

1995 1st poem: Catherine Greenwood
      2nd poem: Sophia Kaszuba
      3rd poem: Neile Graham

1996 1st poem: Patricia Young
      2nd poem: Mildred Tremblay
      3rd poem: Rafi Aaron

1997	1st poem:	Marlene Cookshaw
	2nd poem:	Patricia Young
	3rd poem:	Linda Rogers
1998	1st poem:	Esta Spalding
	2nd poem:	Deanna Yonge
	tied:	Faizal Deen Forrester
	tied:	Richard Lemm

COMPETITION GUIDE LINES

The League of Canadian Poets is a national, not-for-profit and charitable organization and is one of Canada's oldest literary organizations. It was founded by Canadian poets Louis Dudek, Ralph Gustafson, Dorothy Livesay, and Raymond Souster in North Hatley, Quebec, in 1966. The League offers many services to its members and the public, including its three poetry competitions. Among the most prestigious in Canada, our annual competitions discover and encourage new writing talent in this country. For more information about the League of Canadian Poets, please visit the League's website at http://www.poets.ca

Notes for all three competitions: Copyright remains with the poet. Winners will be asked for the first rights to publish their work. The chapbook competition winner will be asked to sign a standard contract for publication. Should an entry be published elsewhere during the course of the contest, we ask that the entrant notify the League immediately. Revisions on any poem will not be accepted after it has been entered. All decisions of the jury are final. Contest is open to Canadian citizens and landed immigrants. Members of the League's National Council, staff or the contest judges or their families are not eligible to enter these competitions.

The League of Canadian Poets' Annual
NATIONAL POETRY CONTEST

We invite all Canadians to participate in the nation's biggest poetry competition: the League of Canadian Poets' annual poetry contest. Entries are now being accepted!

1st prize: $1,000   2nd prize: $750   3rd prize: $500

In addition, fifty poems, including the three winners, will be published in the softcover anthology *Vintage*, published by Ronsdale Press, and sold in bookstores across Canada.

DEADLINE: Entries Postmarked by November 1

Entry Guidelines:
1. Poems may be of any subject matter, type or style. Poems must be previously unpublished and must be your own work.
2. Length of poems must not exceed 75 written lines. There is no limit to the number of poems you may submit. Poetry must be English language.
3. All entries must be typed, single-sided, on plain 8 1/2" x 11" paper. If poems continue onto two or more pages, these should be numbered. Pages should not be stapled together. The title of each poem should appear at the top of the page.
4. Name, address, and phone number must *not* appear on the poems. Entrants must put their name, address and phone number and a four-line biography on a separate sheet of paper, along with the titles of the poems entered.
5. Entries will not be returned, but information on the winners will be sent, if a self-addressed and stamped envelope is included. (Postage costs may go up Jan. 1, so add 1¢ extra postage.)
6. Entry fee is $6 per poem (GST included). Payment must be by cheque or money order, in Canadian funds, payable to The League of Canadian Poets.
7. Winners will be announced on April 6. Announcements will be sent to the media, and the fifty winners will be notified by mail and posted on the League's web-site (www.poets.ca).
8. Address entries to The National Poetry Contest, The League of Canadian Poets, 54 Wolseley Street, Toronto, Ontario, M5T 1A5.

The League of Canadian Poets' Annual
CANADIAN YOUTH POETRY COMPETITION

The League of Canadian Poets invites youth to participate in its annual youth poetry competition. Prizes in each age category:

1st Prize: $500   2nd Prize: $350   3rd Prize: $250   + honourable mentions

The winning poems will be published in the softcover anthology *Vintage*, published by Ronsdale Press, and sold in bookstores across Canada.

DEADLINE: Entries Postmarked by November 15

Entry Guidelines:

1. There are two age categories: Junior, grades 7–9; and Senior, grades 10–12 (OAC in Ontario).
2. Poems may be of any subject matter, type or style. Poems must be previously unpublished and must be your own work.
3. Length of each poem submitted must not exceed one page. There is no limit to the number of poems you may submit. Poetry must be English language.
4. All entries must be typed, single-sided, on plain 8 1/2" x 11" paper. Pages should not be stapled together. The title of each poem should appear at the top of the page.
5. Name, address, and phone number must *not* appear on the poems. You must put your name, age, grade, name of school, your home address and phone number on a separate sheet of paper, along with the titles of the poems entered.
6. Entries will not be returned (always keep a copy of the poems submitted; do not send originals), but information on the winners will be sent, if a self-addressed and stamped envelope is included. (Entrants are reminded that postage costs may go up Jan. 1, so add 1¢ extra postage.)
7. **Entry fees:** $5 per poem or $3 per poem for 3 or more poems or $2.50 per poem for 30 or more poems (group submission rate). Payment must be by cheque or money order, in Canadian funds, payable to The League of Canadian Poets.
8. Teachers are encouraged to take advantage of our group submission rate and make the competition a class project.
9. Winners will be announced on April 6 and posted on the League's web-site (www.poets.ca). Announcements will be sent to the media, and the winners will be notified by mail. Winners will also give a reading during Children's Poetry Week, the second week in April, as part of National Poetry Month celebrations.
10. Address entries to The Canadian Youth Poetry Competition, The League of Canadian Poets, 54 Wolseley Street, Toronto, Ontario, M5T 1A5.

The League of Canadian Poets' Annual
CANADIAN POETRY CHAPBOOK MANUSCRIPT COMPETITION

Canada's largest poetry chapbook competition is inviting Canadians to submit their poetry manuscripts!

1st prize: $1,000 + publication

Selected entrants will also receive honourable mention and a copy of the winning chapbook. In addition, the manuscript of the first-prize winner will be published by the League of Canadian Poets and the author will receive 10 printed and bound copies.

DEADLINE: Entries postmarked by December 1

Entry Guidelines:
1. Poems may be of any subject matter, type or style. Poems must be previously unpublished and must be your own work.
2. Poetry manuscripts of 15 to 24 pages, not more than one poem per page. There is no limit to the number of poetry manuscripts a person may submit. Poetry must be English language.
3. All entries must be typed, single-sided, single spaced, on plain 8 1/2" x 11" paper. Manuscript pages should be titled and numbered.
4. Name, address and phone number must *not* appear on the manuscript. Entrant's name, address and phone number and title(s) of manuscript(s) should be submitted on a separate cover sheet.
5. Entries will not be returned, but information on the winners will be sent, if a self-addressed and stamped envelope is included. (Postage costs may go up Jan. 1, so add 1¢ extra postage.)
6. Entry fee is $15 per chapbook poetry manuscript (GST included). Payment must be by cheque or money order, in Canadian funds, payable to The League of Canadian Poets.
7. Winners will be announced on April 6. Announcements will be sent to the media, and the winners will be notified by mail and posted on the League's web-site (www.poets.ca).
8. Address entries to Canadian Poetry Chapbook Competition, The League of Canadian Poets, 54 Wolseley Street, Toronto, Ontario, M5T 1A5.